Economics in Action

What are Goods and Services?

Carolyn Andrews

Crabtree Publishing
crabtreebooks.com

Crabtree Publishing

crabtreebooks.com 800-387-7650

Author: Carolyn Andrews
Coordinating editor: Chester Fisher
Series editor: Scholastic Ventures
Editor: Amanda Bishop
Proofreaders: Adrianna Morganelli, Crystal Sikkens
Project editor: Robert Walker
Production coordinator: Katherine Berti
Prepress technician: Katherine Berti
Project manager: Santosh Vasudevan (Q2AMEDIA)
Art direction: Dibakar Acharjee (Q2AMEDIA)
Cover design: Ranjan Singh (Q2AMEDIA)
Design: Ruchi Sharma (Q2AMEDIA)
Photo research: Sakshi Saluja (Q2AMEDIA)

Hardcover 978-0-7787-4255-5
Paperback 978-0-7787-4260-9
Ebook (pdf) 978-0-7787-8968-0

Library and Archives Canada Cataloguing in Publication

Andrews, Carolyn, 1951-
What are goods and services? / Carolyn Andrews.

(Economics in action)
Includes index.
ISBN 978-0-7787-4255-5 (bound).--
ISBN 978-0-7787-4260-9 (pbk.)

1. Consumption (Economics)--Juvenile literature. 2. Consumer goods--Juvenile literature. 3. Economics--Juvenile literature. I. Title. II. Series: Economics in action (St. Catherines, Ont.)

HC79.C6A54 2008 j330 C2008-904155-0

Published in Canada
Crabtree Publishing
616 Welland Avenue
St. Catharines, Ontario
L2M 5V6

Published in the United States
Crabtree Publishing
347 Fifth Avenue
Suite 1402-145
New York, NY 10016

Photographs:
Alamy: Canadabrian: p. 28; Peter Titmuss: p. 20 (top)
Bigstockphoto: Chrishg: p. 22
Corbis: Jose Fuste Raga: p. 29
Dreamstime: Lucian Coman: p. 13; David Gilder: p. 18
Istockphoto: Louis Aguinaldo: p. 20 (bottom); Wolfgang Amri: p. 16; Ewen Cameron: p. 6; Anne Clark: p. 27; Lise Gagne: p. 12; Virginia Hamrick: p. 4
Jupiter Images: p. 14; Bananastock: p. 17, 25; Corbis: p. 23; Creatas Images: p. 7; John Lund/Paula Zacharias: p. 15; Thinkstock Images: p. 5; Ale Ventura: p. 24
Photolibrary: Nigel Blythe: cover (center)
Shutterstock: Joy Brown: cover (left); Elena Elisseeva: p. 9; Diana Jo Currier: p. 21 (bottom); Istihza: p. 1; Mikhail Lavrenov: p. 10; Patricia Marks: p. 19; Obak: p. 8 (bottom); Sally Scott: p. 11; Vasca: p. 21 (top); Dave Wetzel: p. 8 (top)

Printed in Canada/092024/CP20240919

Library of Congress Cataloging-in-Publication Data

Andrews, Carolyn.
What are goods and services? / Carolyn Andrews.
p. cm. -- (Economics in action)
Includes index.
ISBN-13: 978-0-7787-4260-9 (pbk. : alk. paper)
ISBN-10: 0-7787-4260-1 (pbk. : alk. paper)
ISBN-13: 978-0-7787-4255-5 (reinforced library binding : alk. paper)
ISBN-10: 0-7787-4255-5 (reinforced library binding : alk. paper)
1. Consumption (Economics)--Juvenile literature. 2. Consumer goods--Juvenile literature. 3. Economics--Juvenile literature. I. Title.
HC79.C6.A537 2009
339.4'8--dc22 2008028978

Contents

Introduction

Adrienne entered the small apartment that would soon be hers. She was about to start college and had found the apartment close to the campus. She was excited about getting it furnished with the items she and her parents had bought during the summer.

Consumers, and Economics

She and her mom had shopped at yard sales, thrift shops, and discount stores to find the things she would **need**. Now the movers carried in a couch, a bed, a table and chairs, and boxes with dishes, silverware, towels, and the rest of her things. Adrienne wanted to add pictures, a television, and rugs to make the apartment more like home.

Adrienne and her family are **consumers**. A consumer is a person who buys and uses things. Everyone eats, wears clothes, and lives in some sort of house. Everyone may not have the newest fashions or brand new furniture, but everyone consumes.

Every consumer is a part of an **economic system**. An economic system is the way things are made, and the way people get those things. For example, in one economic system, what people buy helps manufacturers know what to make and sell. **Economics** is the study of how people make choices to get the things they need and **want**. Needs are the things people must have to live. Wants are the items people like to have but are not needed for life. People need to eat healthy food. People might want toys, cars, bicycles, or chocolate cake.

This family acts as consumers when they eat a meal.

Automobiles are goods that people can buy.

Goods are objects like shoes, houses, and books. Adrienne moved all sorts of goods into her apartment. **Services** are actions or activities one person performs for another. The movers provided a service to Adrienne. Services could also include babysitting, health care, and education. Many people have service jobs in making and selling goods. Other people use goods to perform services.

Many countries get their goods through **trade**. Trade is the voluntary exchange of goods and services between people or countries. Countries trade because they want and need the things that are made in other places.

FACT STOP

Countries want to know how many goods and services their countries make or provide each year. They add the values to get the **gross domestic product (GDP)**.

Needs and Wants

Adrienne's apartment was filled with needs and wants. Rugs, pictures, and a television would make her apartment more comfortable, but she could do without them. Since she could afford a bed, she didn't have to sleep on the floor. But the food in the pantry and refrigerator are needs.

What Do You Need? What Do You Want?

Everyone needs food, water, and shelter. How people meet those needs depends on what is available. People choose after knowing what can be found and how much the needs cost.

All humans need to eat, but everyone eats different foods. Many people in Asia eat rice and vegetables that grow there. In other parts of the world, food is difficult to get because of war or lack of rain. In wealthier countries, most people have plenty of foods to choose from.

Water is important for humans. In richer countries, people build factories, called **water purification plants**, to make sure the water is safe to drink. Poorer countries may not have these.

People need shelter. Around the world, people live in houses, apartments, trailers, grass huts, log cabins, and tents.

People need clean water. This water purification plant provides the service of making clean, safe water.

▲ A bike is a want that many kids would like to have.

Some wants sound like needs. For example, in Houston, having a car is important to many people. This lets them live far away from work and school and get around town. But cars are not needs. People could choose to live close to buses and trains.

Yet companies make all kinds of cars, from under $10,000 to over $50,000. In richer countries, many different kinds of cars are sold. This gives car buyers a lot of choices. People can choose what they can afford to pay.

In poorer countries, the same choice of cars might not be available. If there is not money for factories, steel for cars, or rubber for tires, then even fewer cars are sold. Instead, shoppers have more lower-priced cars and other forms of transportation available.

The choices available depend on the money the consumers have and the resources available.

FACT STOP

Is bottled water a need or a want? After Hurricane Katrina, bottled water was shipped to New Orleans to give to the people still in the area.

Goods of All Kinds

Adrienne looks around her apartment and sees all kinds of goods. These goods can last for many years or for only a short time. **Durable goods** last for many years. **Nondurable** or **consumable goods** last a short length of time. They are meant to be used up or replaced.

Durable Goods

Kitchen appliances are durable goods. Refrigerators, dishwashers, stoves, washers, and dryers usually last up to ten years, and sometimes more. Even if something breaks on an appliance, it can be fixed and last even longer.

Houses last a long time, too. Many houses in the United States built before the Civil War still stand today. Thomas Jefferson started building his house, Monticello, in 1769. Monticello lasted through wars and weather, and today houses a museum.

Some people like to buy a new car every two or three years. This does not mean the car is not usable. Someone else might buy a used car for their teenager to drive. A car will last for many years if the owner properly takes care of it. It is a durable good.

▼ These are both durable goods. And they are both wants!

Consumable Goods

Other goods get replaced because people get tired of them. These goods can be sold at garage sales or donated to charities so that other people can buy and use them. Examples of this would be clothing, shoes, dishes, small appliances, and furniture. They are also durable goods.

Improvements can cause people to replace durable goods. Computers, cell phones, and televisions are all better now than when they were first invented. As a result, many people have replaced the old but working items with new and better goods.

Some durable goods become more valuable over time. Antique cars and furniture are sold at high prices if they are in good condition. Paintings done by artists who lived long ago can be very valuable to art collectors.

Consumable goods are meant to last only a short time. These are goods that people use up, like food and toothpaste. Some consumable goods last longer than others. Fresh foods usually last just a few days. But canned or frozen food can last up to a year. How long shampoo, toothpaste, lotion, and soap last depend on how much is used at a time.

FACT STOP

Some manufacturers make products so that they will not last or so they will go out of style. This is called **built-in obsolescence**. Some clothing styles change each season so people buy new clothes to stay in "style."

Stylish clothes have built-in obsolescence.

Where Do Goods Come From?

Goods and services come from **land**, **labor**, and **capital**. Land, labor, and capital are the **factors of production**. All three are needed for goods and services.

▲ Trees would be considered land because it is a natural resource.

Natural Resources

Natural resources occur naturally in the earth. People take resources from the earth and use them to make something new. Trees are used to make lumber. The lumber is then used to make houses, furniture, and even paper. Iron ore, a mineral, is used to make steel.

Labor is necessary to make the goods. People perform labor and get paid for the work they do. The amount they get paid depends upon the skills and knowledge they use on the job. The person who designs a building makes more money than the person hammering the nails.

Anything that is necessary to make a good is capital. There are two kinds of capital, physical and human. **Physical capital** is the things used to make other goods. **Human capital** is the knowledge and skills that workers have. A farmer's physical capital includes tractors, plows, trailers, and seed. The human capital would be his knowledge and skills of farming. Factories, farmers, bakers, and carpenters are examples of **producers** of goods. A producer is someone who makes or grows goods. Everyone is a consumer, but not everyone is a producer.

FACT STOP

Entrepreneurs are people who take land, labor, and capital and create new goods and services. One such person was Bill Gates. He and his friend, Paul Allen, invented an operating system for personal computers. Their company became known as Microsoft.

▼ It takes labor to plant seeds and harvest the vegetables.

Many Different Kinds of Producers

Consumers want and need many different goods, so producers make many goods. Farmers grow goods on their farms. Other goods are manufactured in factories, at home, or in small businesses.

Farmers grow different kinds of crops. Some crops, like cotton, provide resources to make other goods. Food crops, like grain, vegetables, and fruits, are processed, sold, and shipped to stores all over the United States. Farmers also raise animals as food. Farms provide plants and animals as goods to sell, or as resources to make goods.

There are thousands of factories that take resources and make things out of them. Some factories make shoes, clothing, food, furniture, appliances, computers, fans, and other items. Other factories make machinery to use in the making of goods.

▼ Farmers raise cattle for meat and dairy products.

▲ This tailor makes clothes by hand using a small sewing machine.

Factories make a lot of the same good at one time using an assembly line. The goods move down a conveyor belt. As the goods pass workers along the line, the workers might add a piece to the object or take the good and place it in a box for shipping. Eventually the goods go to stores to sell to consumers.

Factories make goods faster than individuals do, and the goods usually cost less. But there is a drawback. Factories tend to create a lot of waste. This waste pollutes air, water, and land in ways that people working by hand did not.

Many years ago, people made most goods without the use of large machines. Some people still make goods by hand today. For example, tailors use sewing machines, thread, and needles to make or repair clothing for people. They work on only one item at a time. The work is slower but many people think the clothing is better if made by hand.

FACT STOP

In order to build cars faster and cheaper, Henry Ford invented the assembly line. Each worker did one job or task as the car went down the line of workers on a moving belt. Almost anyone could afford to buy a Ford.

Services

Adrienne needed a physical exam before college started. The doctor would listen to her heart, check her throat, and talk to her about any problems or concerns she might have. The doctor is providing a service to Adrienne. A service is an action or activity that one person does for another. Many people provide services in our economy.

People Provide Services

Many people have jobs in the service industry. Teachers, principals, and coaches in schools provide a service to children and parents by helping students learn. Barbers and hair stylists, sales persons, waiters and waitresses, exterminators, housekeepers, bank tellers, and lawyers all provide services. The person using these services pays for them.

Some services are voluntary. This means that people do things for other people because they want to help them. They do not get paid. People volunteer by working in shelters and giving out food, clothing, and blankets. People visit elderly people and read, sing, or do housework for them. Others go to foreign countries to teach and provide medical care.

In 1960, Senator John F. Kennedy made a speech to college students, challenging them to work for peace by living and working in poor countries around the world.

▼ People provide services in many different forms.

▲ Parents often volunteer as coaches to train school students in various sports.

When Kennedy became President of the United States in 1961, the **Peace Corps** came into being. The Peace Corps is a government agency. People of all ages from the United States go to countries that need help. Volunteers work in the schools as teachers and mentors. They help farmers grow crops. They help businesses sell the goods they produce. They teach parents how to provide for their children.

Besides the Peace Corps, the United States has many volunteer agencies. For example, the Red Cross and Salvation Army help people after natural disasters like floods, hurricanes, and earthquakes. Volunteers with the Red Cross and Salvation Army provide temporary shelter, food, clothing, and medical care to those in need.

FACT STOP

The Red Cross trains girls and boys between the ages of 11-15 for babysitting jobs. Parents hire trained babysitters because they can handle an emergency.

Public and Private

Individuals and groups provide many of the goods and services that we use. These goods and services are **private goods**. The government provides other goods and services. These goods and services are **public goods**.

Are Goods and Services Private or Public?

Producers of goods and services go into business in order to make money. **Profit** is the money that they make after paying all of their expenses. The profit gives an **incentive**, or an encouragement, for going into business.

Sometimes, people and groups do not produce goods and services because there is no incentive. It might cost too much to produce the good or service. Instead, the government may provide the good or service.

▼ A doctor in a clinic provides a service. However, patients may not be able to pay for care.

▲ Stores sell clothes to make a profit. These are private goods.

For example, a community may need sidewalks. Everyone in the community wants the sidewalks, but nobody wants to pay for them. The city may tax all of its citizens. The taxes can pay for the sidewalk.

All people use public goods. The public goods and services cost quite a bit. But it makes sense to not charge for these goods and services individually. Instead, the government charges taxes. A tax is a payment to the government that people must pay. These taxes help pay for the public goods and services.

Taxes pay for parks, playgrounds, and some campgrounds. Taxes also pay for highways, roads, and streets.

FACT STOP

The first interstate highway in the United States opened on November 14, 1956, west of Topeka, Kansas. Today, there are over 46,000 miles of interstate highways across the United States.

Taxes and Public Services

Taxes also pay for services. Many of these services help the poor who could not pay for a private service. The services given by the government to the poor are called **welfare**. President Franklin Roosevelt established welfare in the 1930s. The people of the United States struggled during this time. Many people had no work and could not afford to pay for goods or services. President Roosevelt started programs that gave people jobs and helped them pay for needs when they could not on their own.

Today, welfare provides milk and food for families. Children from low-income families can get breakfast and lunch at school for free or at a low cost. If a person loses his job, then he might qualify for money under the unemployment insurance program. Workers hurt on the job can get medical care under a program called workers' compensation. Retired workers who have paid into the Social Security program receive a check each month.

Tax money also pays for police, fire departments, schools, and some hospitals. These services may not be available otherwise. Or they would cost people a lot of money each time they used the service.

FACT STOP

The government first added a tax to the cost of gasoline in 1932. They charged a one cent per gallon tax. Today, the government taxes gas at 18.4 cents per gallon.

▶ The gasoline tax pays for the public service of maintaining and building roads.

If a person chooses not to pay for public goods but uses them anyway, that person is a **free rider**. Free riders benefit from the public good even if they do not pay.

For example, think of a small town with no fire department. Someone living there does not want to pay for a fire department. Other neighbors decide that fire protection is necessary and decide to pay anyway. If the person who does not pay has a fire in his home, the fire department would still put the fire out.

Local taxes pay for the fire department. Everyone is better off if the government provides this service. Governments do not usually wait for people to decide to pay taxes. Instead, they collect taxes from paychecks, sales at stores, and even house payments. This way, people have fewer opportunities to take a "free ride."

The United States is not the only country that collects taxes to pay for public goods. Countries all over the world collect taxes from people to help pay for roads, parks, and aid to the poor.

▲ Taxes pay for firefighters who serve a community.

Scarcity and Surplus

Stores in the United States have shelves that are full of goods of all kinds. Some goods, like shoes, come in many different styles and sizes. Yet, even in the U.S., people deal with **scarcity**. Scarcity means that there are not enough resources to meet all the wants and needs of people. Scarcity is everywhere, all the time.

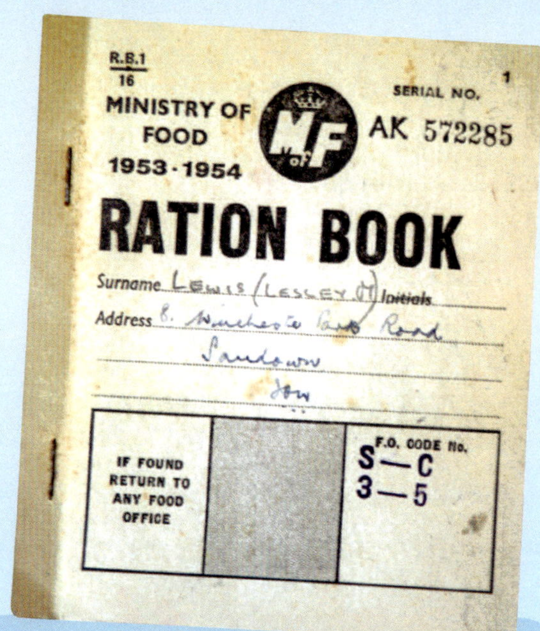

▲ During times of severe shortage, people may need **ration** books for some goods.

Shortages

Not all resources are replaceable. When a miner pulls a mineral from the ground, it is gone forever. Once oil rigs pump the petroleum out of the earth, there will be no more petroleum. There is only a certain amount of land for roads, homes, cities, and crops.

▼ When sugar was scarce, people needed stamps to buy some.

Labor is also scarce. Only a certain number of people can work to produce the goods and services needed. Human and physical capital are also scarce. Since these factors of production are scarce, goods can become scarce.

Because of the scarcity of resources, producers must make decisions about how to use them. They decide which goods and how many of them to make. Producers watch what consumers want to buy. What people want to buy is called **demand**. The number of goods that are available for purchase is the **supply**.

▲ Without a stamp, people could not buy butter or coffee.

Shortages occur when producers do not make enough of a good that consumers want to buy. In other words, the demand is more than the supply. Some shortages last a short time. This means the product people want may not be in the store today, but it might be there next week. Some shortages last a long time.

Throughout history, there have been shortages. During World War II, people in the United States cut back on certain goods so that they could be used in the war. Many goods were not available at all. Metal used to make zippers and toys now went to make guns. Rubber became tires on army trucks instead of tires on cars or bicycles.

Other items were rationed. This means that consumers could only get a certain amount of those goods. People rationed sugar, coffee, meat, butter, and gasoline. In order to buy the items, a person had to have a ration stamp and money. Without the stamp, shoppers could not buy what they wanted or needed.

FACT STOP

In 1973, a comedian made a joke about a shortage of toilet paper in the U.S. Many people took him seriously and bought all the toilet paper they could find. This resulted in a real shortage!

Recent Shortages

During the 1970s, the Organization of Petroleum Exporting Countries (OPEC) banned the shipment of oil to the United States. As a result, the U.S. experienced a shortage of gasoline, heating oil, and other oil products. Over a few months, the price of gasoline doubled and the cost of heating and cooling homes rose. There was not enough gasoline to supply the demand. Gas stations began to ration the gas. The stations even closed on Sundays. The U.S. government asked people to carpool, ride the bus, and use less energy heating and cooling their homes. The government lowered speed limits to save gas. Oil companies began searching for and producing more oil. As a result, the shortage became less severe. The price of gas never got as low as it was in the early 1970s, but more gas was available.

Sometimes, shortages occur because manufacturers make a limited number of the goods. Think of a popular band planning a concert. If the band plans a concert in a building with only 10,000 seats, then they can only sell 10,000 tickets. If more than 10,000 people want a ticket to the concert, the ticket becomes more valuable. The band can charge more money. Many people pay very high prices for tickets to events like this.

Shortages cause people to find new ways to meet their needs and wants. Because of the oil shortage, car companies made cars with better gas mileage. Today, appliances, including air conditioners and heaters, use less energy than those of the 1970s.

▲ A **surplus** of grain is stored in silos and granaries.

▲ Movie and theater tickets can cost more money when the show is in high demand.

When producers make more products than consumers want to buy, there is a surplus. When a surplus of goods exists, producers drop the price of the goods. They offer an incentive for people to buy the excess goods. In this way, the producer is able to sell the extra goods before he produces new ones.

An example of a surplus is wheat. Wheat grows well in many countries. As a result, there is a lot of wheat. Farmers store some of the wheat until the surplus goes down. This keeps the price of the wheat and the products made from wheat high.

FACT STOP

Japan has almost no petroleum resources, so oil is very scarce there. It imports most of its oil from the Persian Gulf countries.

Specialization

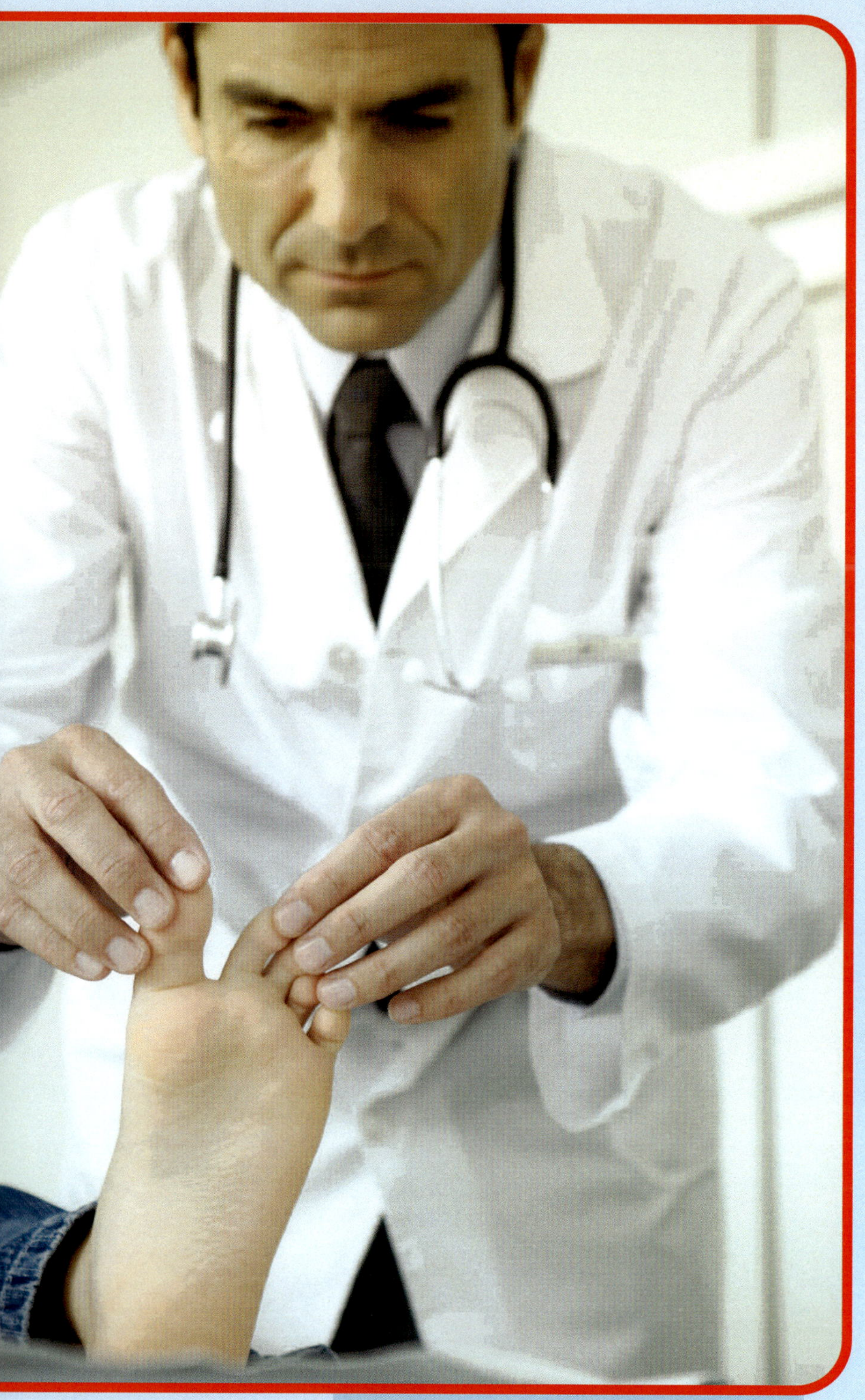

▲ Doctors can specialize in treating certain parts of the body.

Adrienne's college counselor looked over her schedule for the first semester. Everything looked good. The only problem was that Adrienne must decide what field she wants to learn about. The counselor wants Adrienne to **specialize**, or choose only one course of study.

What is a Speciality?

Most people specialize in one kind of work. High school and college teachers usually teach only one subject. For example, a math teacher might teach algebra, geometry, or calculus because these are all math classes. However, this teacher would not teach history.

People in early towns and cities did specific jobs for other people. Some were bakers, tailors, or shoemakers. When people began to work in factories, they usually did only one job. They might run only one kind of machine, or work in the office as a secretary, receptionist, or accountant.

▲ Teachers specialize in the subject they teach.

Specialization has benefits and drawbacks. Specialization helps people to be more efficient. People learn one job and do it well. They can produce more at a cheaper cost. But if a specialization is no longer needed, then people could lose their jobs. These people must learn new jobs or find different employers to use the skills they have. Sometimes, neither option is available.

Countries also specialize in the products they trade. Japan uses robots and specialized workers to produce cars at cheaper prices. The Japanese car companies sell the cars to the U.S. and other countries. In return, Japan buys oil, chemicals, and other products it needs. Countries are dependent upon each other for the goods they need. This is partly due to specialization.

FACT STOP

Poultry farms raise chickens, ducks, turkey, and other fowl, or other birds. Some of the farms specialize in raising poultry only for eggs. Others raise poultry for meat.

Tradeoffs

When Adrienne got ready to apply for college, she considered several things. She wanted to be close to home. She wanted a college with a good academic record. She also wanted a good engineering department. Her family also needed to consider the cost. Adrienne narrowed her choices down to three schools.

Making Decisions

The college she decided to go to was the best choice for her. The colleges she did not decide on were the **tradeoffs**. Tradeoffs are the options given up when a person chooses one action over another. Adrienne's second choice of college was the **opportunity cost**. The opportunity cost is the next best choice after the first choice.

To make a good decision, some people and businesses use a **decision-making grid**. The grid is a table in which they list the choices available, as well as the benefits of each choice.

College	College A	College B	College C
Benefits	• 300 miles from home • Good engineering department • Many friends go there	• 500 miles from home • Fair engineering department • Lower cost • A few friends will go there	• 350 miles from home • Excellent engineering department • Lower cost • No friends there
Decision	College A	College B	College C
Opportunity Cost	College C	College C	College A
Benefits Given Up	• Lower cost	• Close to home • Good engineering department	• Friends • Close to home

For example, Adrienne had three choices for colleges. To make the best choice she made the table on page 26.

Adrienne chose College C. She gave up going to school with her friends in order to pay a lower cost. Her opportunity cost was College A. She would be closer to home but would have to work. For Adrienne, the best choice was College C.

When countries make decisions, they look at all the alternatives and make the best choices for their citizens. Many times the choice involves giving up something because countries, people, and businesses cannot have everything they need or want.

FACT STOP

People buy goods at convenience stores because they are close to where they live. The tradeoff is price. Most convenience stores charge more for their goods.

▼ Students tradeoff fun in order to study for tests.

A Market Economy

Each society must decide how best to use the natural resources it has. Each society must also decide who gets to use the goods and services it produces. The values of the people in the society direct many of these decisions.

Economic Systems

When people value custom and habit, they establish a **traditional economy**. Traditional economies are close-knit farming and hunting communities. These communities do not like change. They put the family and community first. They help each other meet their needs. In times of hardship, such as drought or flood, everyone suffers. In good times, everyone benefits.

In a **centrally planned economy**, or **command economy**, people value economic security. In this type of economy, the central government decides how to use the resources to produce goods and services. Everyone has a job. The government tells farmers what to plant. It tells factories and factory workers what and how much to make. The government sets goals for production. If factories or farmers do not meet the goals, then there are shortages. People often wait in long lines to get goods or go without.

▲ Shoppers make choices based on what is available.

People in a **market economy** value freedom, efficiency, security, and growth. These values lead people to make choices based on what goods and services are available. If people choose to buy the goods, then producers continue to make them. If not, then the producer will make a good that people want. If the goods are not readily available, then exchange or trade is a way of getting the goods needed.

Today, most modern economies are **mixed economies**. In a mixed economy, the market produces goods based on what the consumers want, but the government can step in and make changes if necessary.

The United States has a market economy, but the government makes decisions if necessary. The government passes laws to control trade with other countries. Laws protect the safety of people, keeping stores from selling dangerous goods. An example is the use of lead-based paints on toys. Lead can cause health problems. The government does not allow toy manufacturers to sell toys painted with this type of paint. The government also taxes the people to provide public goods that the market does not provide. These goods are for the use of everyone.

FACT STOP

North Korea and Cuba are command economies. But the governments do not always produce the goods needed by the people. Their people suffer from a lack of goods and services.

Businesses advertise to show what goods and services are available to choose from.

Glossary

built-in obsolescence Making goods so they will last only a certain length of time

capital Any human-made resource used to make the goods or services

centrally planned economy or **command economy** An economic system in which the government decides what is produced and sold

consumable goods Goods that are meant to last only a short time

consumer A person who buys and uses things

decision-making grid A table used to help make good choices

demand What people want to buy

durable goods Goods that are made to last a long time

economic system The way things are made and the way people get those things

economics The study of how people make choices to get the things they need and want

factors of production Three groups of resources, land, labor, and capital, used to make goods and services

free rider A person who uses a service but does not pay

goods Any object a person wants or needs to help them survive

gross domestic product (GDP) The total value of goods and services produced within a country

human capital The knowledge and skills that workers have

incentive An encouragement to act or do something in a specific way

labor The work that goes into making the good or performing the service

land The natural resources that are used to make goods

market economy Economic system that allows the choices people make to determine what is produced and sold

mixed economy Economic system that combines the market economy with limited government involvement

natural resources Materials that occur naturally in the earth, such as minerals, water, trees, and land

need Goods that people need to help them survive

nondurable goods Goods that are meant to last only a short time

opportunity cost The next best choice given up as the result of a decision

Peace Corps Volunteer organization formed in 1961 to help countries in need

physical capital The things used to make other goods

private goods Goods owned by individuals or companies

producer Someone who makes or grows goods

profit The money that a company makes after paying all its expenses

public goods Goods provided by the government and used by all the people of a country

ration To limit the amount of a specific good that a consumer can get

scarcity Limited quantities of resources

service Actions or activities one person performs for another

specialize To devote one's efforts into one activity or area of work

supply The number of goods that are available for purchase

surplus When producers make more products than consumers want to buy

trade The voluntary exchange of goods and services between people or countries

tradeoff All the choices that are given up when one chooses one thing over the others

traditional economy Economic system in which habit or custom determines what is produced and used

want Goods that people like to have but are not necessary for us to live

water purification plants Factories that produce clean water

welfare The services given by the government to the poor

Index

Webfinder

http://www.ja.org/
http://www.ncee.net/ea/index.php
http://www.econedlink.org/
http://library.thinkquest.org/TQ0312380/index.htm